ARMOR SERIES VOL. 7

AF873029

# HALBKETTENFAHRZEUGE

## German Halftrack Vehicles

by
Walter J. Spielberger
and
Uwe Feist

Aero Publishers, Inc.
FALLBROOK, CALIFORNIA

© AERO PUBLISHERS, INC.

1968

*Library of Congress Catalog Card Number*

68-22558

Editor's note: Because the original German specifications and terms used in this book are based on the metric system, the following table is included for convenient referral.

| unit | abbreviation | approximate U.S. equivalent |
|---|---|---|
| 1 centimeter | cm | 0.39 inches |
| 1 kilogram | kg | 2.2046 pounds |
| 1 kilopond | kp | 2.2046 pounds (not affected by atmospheric pressure) |
| 1 kilometer | km | 0.62 miles |
| 1 liter | ltr | 1.057 quarts liquid |
| 1 metric ton | t | 1.1 tons |
| 1 millimeter | mm | 0.04 inches |

*All rights reserved. This book, or parts thereof, must not*

*be reproduced without permission of the publisher.*

**Printed and Published in the United States of America by Aero Publishers, Inc.**

# HALBKETTEN-VEHICLES
## by
## Walter J. Spielberger

Any attempt to complete the story of German army vehicles has to include one of their unique designs, namely the many half-track tractors and armored personnel carriers. These vehicles made up a substantial portion of the hardware inventory and represented for their time an outstanding technical achievement.

Research in this field during World War I was restricted to a few attempts by the companies of Daimler and Benz to create half-track vehicles suitable to negotiate adverse terrain conditions. Daimler's "Marienwagen" and Benz's "Kraftprotze" were representative of these endeavors. Both models were scheduled for mass production when the war came to an end and experience gained from their trials, therefore, limited. The basic research, however, allowed the German High Command to anticipate construction of these kind of vehicles in the early twenties. The demand was great, since not only artillery but also most of the other branches of the Army had need for high speed, off-street tractors to tow their heavy equipment. Since a well-developed road net allowed for quick movements on roads, a solution had to be found to permit these vehicles to also perform satisfactorily under all terrain conditions. Combining the speed of a wheeled vehicle with the cross-country performance of a full-tracked vehicle created an acceptable compromise, whose only real setback was the complexity of the design.

In order to cover all demands for all branches involved, the Ordnance Department decided as early as 1932 to award at least six contracts for half-track vehicles of different sizes. Their rating, however, took into consideration the pulling ability of the vehicles and in its final classification the following units emerged:

| | |
|---|---|
| 1 t half-track series | Parent firm: Demag AG., Wetter/Ruhr |
| 3 t half-track series | Parent firm: Hansa-Lloyd-Goliath AG., Bremen |
| 5 t half-track series | Parent firm: Buessing-NAG, Berlin |
| 8 t half-track series | Parent firm: Krauss-Maffei AG., Muenchen |
| 12 t half-track series | Parent firm: Daimler-Benz AG., Berlin |
| 18 t half-track series | Parent firm: Famo, Breslau |

In 1940, an additional series was included, creating the HK. 100 series, the so.called "Kettenkrad", a combination motorcycle/half-track tractor vehicle of small proportions. With the exception of the HK. 100 series, all other vehicles were almost identical in their basic technical layout. They all had the front end of a conventional wheeled-type vehicle, with the front axle carrying a pair of pneumatic-tired Ackerman-steered front wheels.

Most of the weight of the vehicle, however, was borne on two flexible endless tracks which were supported upon road wheels and which extended the full length of the chassis available rear of the front wheels. Maybach supplied most of the six- or 12-cylinder power plants to propel these vehicles. The steering affected the front wheels first; further turning of the steering wheel brought the steering brakes into action, which were mounted directly in the track final drives. Of special interest also were the tracks, since the anticipated high road speed had asked for lubricated track links and rubber padding of the shoes.

The following is a summary of design history of each one of these vehicles and to give a brief indication as to their usage within the German Wehrmacht:

## HK. 100 series

The smallest tractor of the German Army, designed by the Ordnance Department and its production entrusted to the NSU Werke AG. of Neckarsulm had originally the designation "Versuchs Kfz. 620". Its most popular name, however, was "Kettenkrad", a combination of caterpillar and motorcycle. In fact, it used the front end with wheel and suspension components of a motorcycle and combined it with two scaled-down half-track suspension units. Equipped with the well-known 1.5 litre power plant of the Opel "Olympia" passenger car, a water-cooled four-cylinder motor with 36 HP, it reached a top speed of 80 km an hour. Introduced for the first time to troops on the fifth of June, 1941, it carried the official nomenclature, "kleines Kettenkraftrad" (Sd. Kfz. 2). Used mainly for supply purposes, it was also intended to pull light artillery pieces, especially for paratroop units. It remained in production until 1944. Its components were also used to build the full-tracked, radio-controlled demolition vehicle, called "Springer", which saw limited action during the last month of the war.

The limited payload of the "Kettenkrad" initiated a similar design of somewhat larger proportions, designated "grosses Kettenkraftrad". It was supposed to carry five persons instead of the three of the standard vehicle. This HK. 102 was to be equipped with a 2 litre four-cylinder Stump K 20 engine, capable of an output of 65 HP. It never reached production stage.

## 1 t Half-track Series

Design of this vehicle started as early as 1934 by the Demag AG. of Wetter/Ruhr. Starting with the proto types "D 11 1" and "D 11 2", both equipped with the BMW six-cylinder "315" engine, the preliminary work ended with the type "D 11 3" in 1936. This unit was extensively troop-tested and showed marked improvement because of the new type "319" power plant. Some of these vehicles came equipped with bullet-proof tires. Intended to tow either the 37 mm AT gun, the light 7.5 cm infantry howitzer 18, the heavy 15 cm infantry howitzer 33, or the ammunition trailer 32, the vehicle was soon readied for production. It appeared in 1937 as pre-production type "D 6", having the Maybach "NL 38" six-cylinder power plant replacing the former BMW engine. As soon as the standard Maybach "HL 42" was available in 1939, the designation was changed to "D 7". This vehicle remained in production until 1944 and carried the official name "leichter Zugkraftwagen 1t" (Sd. Kfz. 10). On the 20th of December, 1942, the German Army had 11,116 of these vehicles in their inventory. Main suppliers of these units were the companies of Mechanische Werke Cottbus in Silesia, and the Saurerwerke of Vienna, Austria. Intensive attempts were also made to incorporate the industrial potential of the French automotive industry for the half track development. The companies of Peugeot, Renault, Lorraine, Panhard and Simca were involved. The basic vehicle was modified for many purposes, the main conversion being a gas detector vehicle, a decontamination vehicle and a self-propelled mount for the 2 cm AA gun. Some of the vehicles used for this purpose had armored cabs. Also mounted were 5 cm AT guns to provide more mobility for these weapons. In 1939, investigation revealed the possibility of mounting an armored superstructure to this vehicle. In order to compensate for the limited payload of the basic vehicle, the chassis was shortened by eliminating one road wheel per side. While Demag provided the modified chassis, Buessing-NAG of Berlin developed the armored body. The vehicle, thus created, was named "leichter Schuetzenpanzerwagen" (Sd. Kfz. 250) and appeared over the years in at least ten different versions, ranging from an armored personnel carrier to radio and communication vehicles, to mortar carriers and support vehicles mounting the 75 mm guns. In addition, Sturmgeschuetz units received, as early as 1940, armored observations vehicles (Sd. Kfz. 253) and armored ammunition carriers (Sd. Kfz. 252) based upon this vehicle. Lightly armored with 14.5 mm plates in front and 8 mm plates on the sides, with open roofs they had a fighting weight of up to 4.6 metric tons. While chassis were built by both Demag and Mechanische Werke of Cottbus, assembly took place at Evens & Pistor of Helsa in Thuringia. Most of the armor was supplied by Bismarckhuette of Upper Silesia.
Concluding the development of this series was the type "D 8", which appeared on the drawing boards in 1939. A greatly increased top speed of 74 km per hour characterized this development.

## HK. 300 series

Parallel to the development of the 1 t vehicle run was a design of the Adlerwerke AG of Frankfurt. One prototype of this "kleine Zugmaschine HK. 301" was delivered on the 16th of August, 1941. Four additional prototypes followed. An order for an O-series of 50 units was placed but later cancelled, since the necessity for such a vehicle could no longer be substantiated. All of these vehicles were equipped with Maybach four-cylinder prototype engines.

## Leichter Wehrmachtsschlepper

In an attempt to simplify the somewhat complicated technical design of all German half-track vehicles, an order was placed by Hitler on May 7, 1942, to create "locust-like" tractors which would serve satisfactorily under the adverse weather conditions experienced in Russia. Production was supposed to be started in spring of 1943, for a light military tractor designed by Adler. The first two prototypes appeared by the end of 1942 and were equipped with the Maybach "HL 30" four-cylinder power plant. The chassis was greatly simplified and sported dry-pin tracks. Armor for the cabs was optional, since one of the intended uses was as a self-propelled mount. The third prototype left Adler in 1944, now equipped with the standard "HL 42" engine. The development ended with the type "HK 305", whose blueprint indicated that it was to be equipped with a Maybach "Olvar" pre-selective transmission.

# 3 t Half-track series

The development of this series was also initiated in 1934, when the Hansa-Lloyd-Goliath AG of Bremen created the type "HL kl 2". An improved version appeared in 1936, carrying the designation "HL kl 3". This time also saw several attempts to move the power train toward the end of the vehicle, to make it able to adopt an armored superstructure. This research resulted in the prototypes "HL kl 4 (H)" in 1936.

One of these chassis was armored by Rheinmetall of Duesseldorf by order of the Ordnance Department in 1935. It was called "3.7 Selbstfahrlafette L/70" and carried its armament in a 360° traverse turret. Total weight of the vehicle was 6 metric tons. It was intended as a mobile anti-tank weapon. Prototypes of the "H 8 (H)" design concluded this development.

The tractor development produced in 1937 the pre-production model "HL kl 5", still equipped with the Borgward "L 3500 L" six cylinder power plant. Starting in 1939, the final production model appeared, now mounting the Maybach "HL 38" engine, which was subsequently replaced by the "HL 42" motor. By December 20, 1942, 4,209 of these vehicles were in troop inventory; they remained in substantial numbers with German units until the end of the war. Built by Borgward of Bremen (former Hansa-Lloyd-Goliath), Hanomag of Hannover, Adler of Frankfurt, Auto-Union of Chemnitz and the Skodawerke of Pilsen, these vehicles were given the official designation, "leichter Zugkraftwagen 3 t" (Sd. Kfz. 11). They served mainly with artillery units towing the 105 mm light field howitzer or an ammunition trailer. During the later war years, it was frequently used to tow the 75 mm and 88 mm AT guns. Other versions were mainly issued to chemical warfare outfits. Towards the end of the war, the vehicle received a wooden loading platform, and its fuel supply was increased to 160 litres.

The chassis of this tractor served as a basis for the most numerous armored vehicles of the German Wehrmacht. With the companies of Hanomag responsible for the chassis and Buessing-NAG for the armored superstructure, a vehicle was created which formed the backbone of armored infantry units throughout the war. Originally called "mittlerer gepanzerter Mannschaftskraftwagen" (Sd. Kfz. 251) and later "mittlerer Schuetzenpanzerwagen", it appeared in as many as 23 official versions. Almost 15,000 of these vehicles were built during the war. Its production was continued after the war in Czechoslovakia, and the vehicle is still being used today, only slightly altered under the designation "OT 810". With a basic frontal armor of 14.5 mm, a side armor of 8 mm, open top, it had a fighting weight of approximately 7 metric tons. To satisfy the demand, several companies were engaged in its production. Adler of Frankfurt, Auto-Union of Chemnitz, Hanomag of Hannover, Borgward of Bremen, and Skoda of Pilsen supplied chassis, while Ferrum of Laurahuette, Schoeller & Bleckmann of Muerzzuschlag, Bohemia of Boehmisch-Leipa and Steinmueller of Gummersbach provided the armored superstructures. Final assembly took place at Weserhuette of Bad Oeynhausen, Wumag of Goerlitz and F. Schichau AG. of Elbing.

Various attempts were made throughout the years to replace the existing half-track models with improved versions. A standard 3 t class vehicle, supposed to replace all previous models, was called "H 7" and looked very similar to the Sd. Kfz. 251. Both Hanomag and Demag were engaged in the development replacement vehicles, called the HK. 600 series. Various prototypes, soft-skinned and armored, were conceived but did not materialize owing to the economic condition in Germany and the fact that other, more pressing needs made any exploitation of technical improvements impossible. Advanced technical innovations like disc brakes, frame-body assemblies, and fully-automatic transmissions had to be shelved, since production capacities could not be activated. Only drawings and prototypes marked the end of the most promising HK. 600 series.

The standard vehicles remained in production, their exterior altered to accommodate most modern production methods. In 1943, the bodies of the 1 t and 3 t armored personnel carriers were modified to cut down on production man hours. Raw material shortages forced an attempt to replace the rubber cushions of the lubricated tracks with steel caps. Negative experience cancelled this experiment. Both tractor and armored personnel carrier versions remained in production until the war ended.

# 5 t Half-track series

Buessing-NAG of Berlin-Oberschoeneweide was responsible for this series and presented, after several prototypes, the first production model, "BN 1 4" in 1934. Intended for both artillery and engineering outfits, this unit was equipped with a Maybach "NL 35" six-cylinder engine. At the same time, this unit also went into production at Krauss-Maffei in Munich, carrying the type designation "KM 1 4".

Three of these vehicles were converted by Rheinmetall-Borsig to self-propelled mounts moving the power plant to the rear of the vehicle. 20 mm armor protected a crew of four. Starting as early as 1934, it carried a most advanced 75 mm gun in a rotating turret. With a length of L/40.8, it was intended to become

the carrier of offensive fire power for cavalry units. All three versions were different in height, length and width, and total weight was up to six tons. One of these prototypes saw action in North Africa.
1935 saw an improved version, the "BN 1 5", still equipped with the same engine. Daimler-Benz participated in this production run, naming their vehicle "DB 1 5". Without any outside differences, the model "BN 1 7" appeared in 1936, having now the Maybach "NL 38" engine, with 100 BHP. Daimler-Benz again produced their version, calling it "DB 1 7". The following model was changed considerably, both in appearance and layout. Designated "BN 1 8" (the Daimler-Benz model "DB 1 8"), this unit had an increased track on the ground length and a re-designed body. Buessing built 465 and Daimler-Benz 272 units of this series. 1939 saw the introduction of the final version of this unit, called "BN 9", and its modified version, "BN 9b", differentiated only by a different braking system. They had, however, a more powerful engine, Maybach "HL 54", with 115 BHP. Buessing-NAG produced a total of 687 units, and on the 20th of December, 1942, 2,061 of these 5 t half-tracks were in inventory. Their official nomenclature, was: "mittlerer Zugkraftwagen 5 t" (Sd. Kfz. 6). The basic vehicle was used in engineering outfits to tow their bridging equipment trailers, while Sd. Kfz. 6/1 was used by artillery outfits to tow the 105 mm light field howitzer 18. Another production model was the Sd. Kfz. 6/2, a self-propelled mount for the 37mm AA gun. Weighing 10.4 tons, it carried a crew of seven. An order by the Ordnance Department made Alkett of Berlin produce an anti-tank self-propelled mount for the 7.62 cm Russian AT gun, Pak 36 (r). Using the 5 t Zgkw chassis, it had a crew of five and a total weight of 10.5 metric tons, was lightly armored and was named "Diana". One prototype of a series of nine was sent to Libya, where it was captured by the British. Production of the 5 t vehicles ceased in 1943 when it was replaced by the "schwere Wehrmachtsschlepper", built by both Buessing-NAG and Ringhoffer-Tatra. High command judged the demand for this vehicle on July 27, 1942, to be 7,484 units, and starting in the spring of 1943, a monthly production of 150 units was anticipated. Production, however, did not start before December, 1943, when only five units were actually produced. Only a limited number of "Wehrmachtsschlepper" saw action. Equipped with the Maybach "HL 42", it had a greatly-simplified suspension system and dry-pin tracks. Mainly intended as a supply vehicle, armored versions were used as self-propelled mounts for both the 37 mm Flak 43 and the ten-barrelled rocket launcher 42.
Since production of this vehicle was consistently delayed, Daimler-Benz was asked to convert some of their 4.5 standard trucks to half-track vehicles. By removing the rear axle and the power train and replacing it with the running gear of the Panzer II, a vehicle was created which supplemented the 3 t "Maultier" series, using Opel, Ford, and Magirus trucks. Called "Gleisketten Lkw 4½ t, offen" (Maultier), these units remained in production until 1944. Some of the later vehicles used a simplified Carden-Loyd suspension system.

## 8 t Half-track series

The company responsible for the development of this series was the Krauss-Maffei's AG. of Munich-Allach. Already in 1928, this company had made attempts to equip one of their wheeled tractors of the type "MS" with caterpillar tracks instead of the rear wheels. Their first model, based upon the design of the Ordnance Department, the type "KM m 7" of type "1934", appeared late in 1933. It was immediately followed by the type "KM m 8". which had an increased track length on the ground and was equipped with the Maybach "HL 52" six-cylinder engine. Participating in this production run were both Buessing-NAG (type BN m 8) and Daimler-Benz (type DB m 8). The following type "KM m 9", appearing for the first time in 1936, was exclusively Krauss.Maffei's responsibility and now had installed the Maybach "HL 57". Almost identical in appearance was the following model, designated "KM m 10", which left the production lines by the end of 1936. It had again an improved Maybach engine, namely the "HL 62", with an output of 140 BHP. Hansa-Lloyd-Goliath AG of Bremen produced 222 units of the same vehicle under their designation "HL m 10". The official nomenclature assigned read: "mittlerer Zugkraftwagen 8 t" (Sd. Kfz. 7). 1937 saw the introduction of the final model of this series, called "KM m 11", or their counterpart, produced by Borgward as "HL m 11". These units had the track length on the ground increased to 2235 mm. Army inventory on December 20, 1942, saw 3,262 of these vehicles in action, mainly used to tow the 10 cm guns or the 15 cm heavy howitzers of artillery units, while Flak outfits used it as prime mover for the 88 mm AA gun.
Some versions were utilized as self-propelled mounts for either the quadruple 20 mm AA gun 38 (Sd. Kfz. 7/1) or for the 37 mm Flak 36 (Sd. Kfz. 7/2). Some of these vehicles received partial armor for both engine compartment and cab. Late in the war, the Austrian Saurer Werke AG. of Vienna participated in the production of these units.

Alkett of Berlin received an order on the 14th of August, 1941, to use 8 t Zgkw components to create a Panzerjaeger vehicle mounting the Russian 7.62 cm Pak. The vehicle was armored and had the designation, "Artemis".
By 1940, Krauss-Maffei engaged in the prototype production of the "HK. 900" series, a vehicle intended to replace both the 5 t and 8 t half track tractors. Four + 30 units were ordered, with anticipated delivery from February through December, 1941. Thirty prototypes were actually completed, out of which 15 were of the type "HK. 905", with OLVAR transmissions and "Einheit" suspension system.
The interest created by these units is reflected in the fact that the British Ministry of Supply ordered the Vauxhall Motors Ltd. of Luton, Beds, to copy the 8 t half-track for production in England. Six prototypes of the vehicle "BT" were produced and equipped with two each of the standard 214 cu. inch truck engines. Fiat of Italy attempted a similar design, but did not proceed beyond the prototype stage.
Some of the original 8 t Zgkw. appeared with V 2 rocket outfits and served with armored superstructures as fire guidance units. They also were used to tow the launching platform.

# 12 t Half-track series

Basing their experience upon the design of the "Marienwagen" of World War I, the Daimler-Benz AG of Berlin-Marienfelde was first to build one of the new half-track vehicles. It was identified as type "ZD 5" and already appeared in early 1931, built under order by the Russian government, which at that time collaborated closely with military establishments in Germany. 1934 saw the introduction of its improved version, the type "DB s 7". It equipped heavy artillery units until 1936, when a new model, called "DB s 8", appeared. Still mounting the Maybach 12-cylinder "DSO 8" power plant, with an output of 150 BHP, it had already the appearance of the final model. These were the types "DB 9", built during 1938 and 1939, and the model "DB 10", in production until 1944. Both models came equipped with the Maybach 12-cylinder "HL 85" engine. Their official designation: "schwerer Zugkraftwagen 12 t" (Sd. Kfz. 8). Intended to tow either the 15 cm gun 16, the 15 cm gun 18, the 21 cm mortar 18, or the 10.5 cm Flak, these vehicles were also built by Krupp of Muehlhausen and Skoda of Pilsen. The Czech Army still used them in 1955. Inventory figures of December 20, 1942, show 1,615 of these vehicles with Wehrmacht units.
Daimler-Benz received an order in 1940 to investigate the possibility for a new series of half-tracks called "HK 1601". They were intended to replace both the existing 12 t and 18 t vehicles. Four + 30 units were ordered, with delivery starting in February of 1941. Their final designation was "HK. 1604".

# 18 t Half-track series

Last but not least, the heaviest vehicle of the production program was the "schwerer Zugkraftwagen 18 t" (Sd. Kfz. 9), designed and built by Fahrzeug- und Motorenbau GmbH (FAMO) of Breslau. 1936 saw the introduction of the pre-production model "FM gr 1", which was followed in 1938 by the model "F 2". Both units were quite identical in appearance and came equipped with the Maybach "HL 98" power plant. Intended as prime mover for the 24 t lowbed trailer to retrieve disabled tanks, it was also used for towing heavy artillery pieces, such as the 24 cm gun K 3 and the 12.8 cm Flak 40. The final model "F 3" was introduced in 1939 and stayed in production until 1944. It was now propelled by the Maybach "HL 108" engine, developing 270 BHP. 855 of these vehicles were in troop inventory on December 20, 1942.
All the way through 1944, these vehicles served as the standard tank retriever of the German Army. Some of them came equipped with heavy spades to increase their pulling ability. With the introduction of heavier armored fighting vehicles, such as the "Panther" and the "Tiger", their power proved to be inadequate. Sometimes up to three of these vehicles were needed to move one tank. The armored recovery vehicle, "Bergepanther", took over their task, starting in 1943. With the order of April 19, 1940, the company of Bilstein equipped the 18 t Zgkw with a crane of 6 t capacity and created a unit called Sd. Kfz. 9/1. A gasoline-electric driven crane of 10 t capacity received the designation Sd. Kfz. 9/2.
Fourteen of the 18 t Zgkw vehicles were converted to self-propelled mounts in June and July, 1943. They received light armor and carried the 88 mm Flak 37. For this purpose, the torsion bar suspension had to be reinforced, since a total weight of 25 tons was anticipated.
They were to carry 40 rounds of ammunition. Conversion took place at the Weserhuette of Bad Oeynhausen.
A final design, designated "F 4", marked the end of the German half-track development. It was to carry the new Maybach six-cylinder engine, "HL 116". The project, however, was never completed.

The last to be developed but the smallest unit of the entire half-track production was the NSU HK 101, also called the "Kettenkrad."

## KLEINES KETTENKRAFTRAD (Sd. Kfz. 2) Type "HK 101"

| | | |
|---|---|---|
| CREW | 3 | |
| COMBAT WEIGHT | 1560 kp | |
| LENGTH | 3000 mm | |
| WIDTH | 1000 mm | |
| HEIGHT | 1200 mm | |
| MAXIMUM SPEED | 80 km/h | |
| MAXIMUM RANGE | 250 km | |
| ARMAMENT | None | |
| AMMUNITION | — — | |
| ARMOR | FRONT | |
| | SIDE | |
| | TOP | = W/O |
| | REAR | |
| ENGINE | 1. 5 ltr. Opel Olympia 4 cyl. gasoline 36 BHP | |
| TRANSMISSION | FORWARD 3 x 2 REVERSE 1 x 2 | |
| FUEL CAPACITY | 42 ltr. | |
| TRACK WIDTH | 170 mm | |
| MANUFACTURER | NSU WERKE AG., Neckarsulm | |

Normally intended to supply units under adverse weather conditions in Russia, it was also used to tow light artillery pieces for paratroop units. A crew of three was anticipated.

One of the early prototypes of the 1 t series, called Type D 11 2, was still equipped with the BMW engine. It served as a test bed for further production models.

The pre-production model was the Type D 6, later on renamed D 7, which remained in production until 1945. It was the standard light prime mover of the German Army. Normally a crew of 8 was carried. It was a highly-complicated design, with a Maybach preselective transmission providing sufficient flexibility but complicating maintenance.

The 1 t half-track also served as a self-propelled mount for the 2 cm Flak 38, and was called Sd. Kfz. 10/4. It was the main equipment of the Army anti-aircraft units.

## LEICHTER ZUGKRAFTWAGEN 1 t (Sd. Kfz. 10) Type "D7"

| | | | |
|---|---|---|---|
| CREW | 8 | | |
| COMBAT WEIGHT | 4900 kp | | |
| LENGTH | 4750 mm | | |
| WIDTH | 1840 mm | | |
| HEIGHT | 1620 mm | | |
| MAXIMUM SPEED | 65 km/h | | |
| MAXIMUM RANGE | 285 km | | |
| ARMAMENT | None | | |
| AMMUNITION | — — | | |
| ARMOR | FRONT | | |
| | SIDE | | |
| | TOP | = W/O | |
| | REAR | | |
| ENGINE | Maybach "HL 42 TRKM" 6-cyl. gasoline 100 BHP | | |
| TRANSMISSION | Maybach | FORWARD 7 | REVERSE 3 |
| | Pre-selective | | |
| FUEL CAPACITY | 110 ltr. | | |
| TRACK WIDTH | 240 mm | | |
| MANUFACTURER | Demag, Wetter-Adler, Frankfurt - Buessing-NAG, Berlin - Mechanische Werke Cottbus - MIAG, Braunschweig - M.N.H. Hannover - Saurer, Vienna | | |

Some of the vehicles had lightly armored driver cabs to protect the crew. During action, however, the gun crew was always exposed to attacking aircraft. This in itself and the fact that the fire power of the 2 cm gun left much to be desired rendered these vehicles inadequate.

It was also attempted to mount the 37 mm gun on this vehicle, together with a makeshift armor plating, which was mounted to protect both the vehicle and the crew.

Since the 37 mm gun proved soon to be inadequate, some of these units were equipped with the 5 cm Pak 39, a weapon which saw action at the beginning of the Russian campaign.

A unit equipped with 1 t half-track vehicles in action in France in 1940. Leading the column is the armored personnel carrier version, while the two following units are of the tractor type. The third vehicle tows an ammunition trailer for support of the heavy infantry howitzer, which was mounted on a self-propelled Panzer I chassis.

The standard light armored personnel carrier, intended for a squad of 6, shown here crossing a bridge toward the end of 1944.

This unit abandoned in North Africa was used as a company leader vehicle and mounted the 37 mm anti-tank gun.

This unit was intended as a support vehicle for the squad vehicles which were normally only equipped with machine guns. The 37 mm gun was soon to be replaced with the 75 mm short-barrelled tank gun to provide more effective fire power.

Some of the squad leader vehicles also came equipped with the 28 mm taper bore heavy anti-tank rifle, which was mounted behind a sandwich-type armored shield.

Adverse weather conditions in Russia forced abandonment of the wheeled armored reconnaissance vehicles and their substitution with half-tracked units. The Sd. Kfz. 250/9 mounted the turret of the light armored carrier Sd. Kfz. 222.

It carried the 2 cm KwK 38 and one machine gun. Both weapons could also be utilized against aircraft. The unit shown has been captured by U.S. troops in Italy.

The first appearance of the light armored personnel carrier was during the French campaign in 1940. Here, a column of German armored vehicles is seen bypassing obstacles of the Maginot line. The vehicle in front is the light armored personnel carrier, while the unit ahead of it is the standard medium armored personnel carrier of the German Army.

Artillery units used a similar vehicle for observation purposes. This unit has been knocked out by a mine in Africa. It clearly shows the traverse leaf suspension arrangement of the front axle.

Marshal Rommel used one of these units as a command car in Africa. Additional wireless sets were installed and the vehicle was equipped with the typical frame antenna, which was used on many German radio communication vehicles during this time. This vehicle is depicted in our color page.

Sturmgeschuetz units were equipped with ammunition carriers based upon the 1 t half-track chassis. This unit, developed by Wegmann, was used only in limited numbers.

# LEICHTER, GEPANZERTER KRAFTWAGEN (Sd. Kfz. 250)

## Type "D 7p"

| | | | |
|---|---|---|---|
| CREW | 6 | | |
| COMBAT WEIGHT | 5800 kp | | |
| LENGTH | 4560 mm | | |
| WIDTH | 1945 mm | | |
| HEIGHT | 1660 mm | | |
| MAXIMUM SPEED | 65 km/h | | |
| MAXIMUM RANGE | 320 km | | |
| ARMAMENT | According to use | | |
| AMMUNITION | — — | | |
| ARMOR | FRONT | 14.5 mm | |
| | SIDE | 8 mm | |
| | TOP | 8 mm | |
| | REAR | 8 mm | |
| ENGINE | Maybach "HL 42 TRKM" 6 cyl. gasoline 100 BHP | | |
| TRANSMISSION | Maybach | FORWARD 7 | REVERSE 3 |
| | Pre-selective | | |
| FUEL CAPACITY | 140 ltr. | | |
| TRACK WIDTH | 240 mm | | |
| MANUFACTURER | Demag, Wetter - Evens & Pistor, Helsa | | |

MITTLERER ZUGKRAFTWAGEN 8 t (St. Kfz. 7)

MITTLERER SCHUETZENPANZERWAGEN (Sd. Kfz. 251/1)
Ausfuehrung A

MITTLERER SCHUETZENPANZERWAGEN (Sd. Kfz. 251/1)
Ausfuehrung D

# LEICHTER SCHUETZENPANZERWAGEN (Sd. Kfz. 250)

Picture illustrates Sd. Kfz. 250/3, a radio command vehicle used by Field Marshal Erwin Rommel in North Africa.

The "Leichte Wehrmachts Schlepper," a vehicle of greatly simplified design, appeared only as prototypes.

All these prototypes came equipped with armored cabs, since they were intended to be used as self-propelled mounts for anti-aircraft weapons. No production followed.

The initial model of the 3 t half-track series was the Type HL K1 2 built in 1934. It pointed toward the development of a rather substantial number of vehicles in this class.

The following model, the type Kl 3, already had the typical radiator of all German half-track vehicles. Only a limited number of these prototypes were procured.

## LEICHTER ZUGKRAFTWAGEN 3 t (Sd. Kfz. 11) Type "H Kl 6"

| | |
|---|---|
| CREW | 8 |
| COMBAT WEIGHT | 7200 kp |
| LENGTH | 5550 mm |
| WIDTH | 2000 mm |
| HEIGHT | 2150 mm |
| MAXIMUM SPEED | 52. 5 km/h |
| MAXIMUM RANGE | 275 km |
| ARMAMENT | — — |
| AMMUNITION | — — |
| ARMOR | FRONT<br>SIDE<br>TOP = W/O<br>REAR |
| ENGINE | Maybach "HL 42 TUKRM" 6 cyl. gasoline 100 BHP |
| TRANSMISSION | Hanomag FORWARD 4 x 2 REVERSE 1 x 2 |
| FUEL CAPACITY | 110 Litres |
| TRACK WIDTH | 280 mm |
| MANUFACTURER | Borgward, Bremen - Hanomag, Hannover - Adler, Frankfurt - Auto-Union, Chemnitz - Skoda, Prague |

Some of these units were equipped with rear engines, and Reinmetall provided one with an armored superstructure. It carried a high velocity 37 mm gun L/70 in a rotating turret. They were intended to provide anti-tank protection for cavalry units.

The pre-production type HL K1 5, produced in 1936, already had the appearance of the final model but was still equipped with the Borgward 3.5 litre engine.

The production model was called H K1 6 and was the standard 3 t prime mover mainly intended to tow the 105 mm light field howitzer. During the war, it also towed the 75 and 88 mm anti-tank guns.

The Africa Corps also used a number of these units as prime movers for artillery units and other supply purposes.

The engines of these units were altered slightly to compensate for the conditions encountered in desert warfare.

"Nebelwerfer" units of the German Army not only used 3 t half-track tractors to tow the rocket launcher but also to carry the ammunition. This vehicle shows the arrangement of the ammunition racks.

Some of these vehicles were equipped with an ambulance body and used by the German Coast Guard for the rescue of stranded crew members.

The first medium armored personnel carriers were issued to the Panzer divisions in 1939. They were to become one of the most numerous fighting vehicles of the German Army.

Three versions, Ausf. A, **B** and C had appeared by 1940 and were used by almost every branch of the German Army.

Ausf. A and B had a two-piece front plate and in their original form a machine gun without an armored shield. This version is already equipped with the new gun mount.

Wire rolls carried on the front of the vehicles, were used to block streets against full-tracked vehicles. The original front plate can be seen in this picture.

A command vehicle crossing a river in France, in 1940. This unit was used by staff officers and served as communication links between Panzer units.

Ausf. C, as shown, had a straight front plate. This unit was used by engineering outfits, where it served many purposes.

Another engineering outfit carrying bridging equipment for crossing anti-tank ditches. The improved armor of the motor compartment is clearly visible.

In crossing obstacles, the non-driven front wheels were often freely exposed, since most of the weight of the vehicle was carried on the tracked portion of the suspension.

Another engineering vehicle towing a 28 mm tapered-bore anti-tank gun. This weapon was soon discontinued in production, since tungsten steel could not be made available for its shells.

The medium armored personnel carrier also served as a flame thrower tank, having a total of three throwers carried in the vehicle, two of which were mounted on either side. A portable unit was carried on the inside for close-range attacks. The machine gun mounted in the armor shield is an MG 42.

Serving as a support vehicle, the unit also mounted the 75 mm short-barreled tank gun, the original main armament of the Panzer IV. This picture shows the crew cleaning the barrel during action in Russia.

Starting in 1943, the "D" version of the armored personnel carrier had a much-simplified superstructure. This unit is a mortar carrier, with the bottom plate carried on the front of the vehicle.

A Panzergrenadier unit on its way to the front. The new body style of the "D" version can be seen.

During field trials, one of the personnel carriers has camouflaged itself by using smoke candles.

This rear view shows the mounting of the second MG 42 in a swivel mount, which also allowed for defense against low-flying aircraft. Note the double entry door.

This view exposes the front axle arrangement of the medium armored personnel carrier, and shows the rigid axle beam supported by a transverse leaf spring.

This interior shot shows the arrangement of the seats for the infantry squad. The mounting for both machine guns and the open top arrangement of the vehicle are visible. Accessibility to the unit was good, since the crew could dismount readily, even while the vehicle was in motion.

The containers mounted on both sidewalls contained tools and other stowage items.

Older models had an armored flap which provided visibility to the side. This unit, an earlier model, is shown approaching a burning village in Russia.

Vision for the driver to the sides of the "D" version was secured by means of an unprotected vision slit in those later models.

An armored engineering outfit equipped with late-model SPW's, showing the crew and the bridging equipment carried on both sides of the vehicle. Note also the additional fuel containers mounted to the sidewalls.

# MITTLERER, GEPANZERTER KRAFTWAGEN (Sd. Kfz. 251)

## Type "H Kl 6p"

| | | | |
|---|---|---|---|
| CREW | 12 | | |
| COMBAT WEIGHT | 8500 kp | | |
| LENGTH | 5800 mm | | |
| WIDTH | 2000 mm | | |
| HEIGHT | 2100 mm | | |
| MAXIMUM SPEED | 52. 5 km/h | | |
| MAXIMUM RANGE | 300 km | | |
| ARMAMENT | According to use | | |
| | —— | | |
| ARMOR | FRONT | 14. 5 mm | |
| | SIDE | 8 mm | |
| | TOP | 8 mm | |
| | REAR | 8 mm | |
| ENGINE | Maybach "HL 42 TUKRM" 6 cyl. gasoline 100 BHP | | |
| TRANSMISSION | Hanomag | FORWARD 4 x 2 | REVERSE 1 x 2 |
| FUEL CAPACITY | 160 Litres | | |
| TRACK WIDTH | 280 mm | | |
| MANUFACTURER | F. Schichau, Elbing - Weserhuette, Bad Oeynhausen - Wumag, Goerlitz | | |

To protect Panzergrenadier units from low-flying Allied fighter bombers, this version of the 3 t half-track was created to allow for defense against both aircraft and ground targets.

Troop trial with these units started in 1943. The vehicles, however, did not reach front troops in substantial numbers.

It should be noted that to accommodate the 2 cm gun in a 360° traverse, the body had to be altered considerably.

The model HKp 606 was supposed to replace all existing armored personnel carriers by 1944.

It never went, however, beyond the prototype stage, since limitations in production facilities did not allow for the production of new weapons.

One of the first models of the 5 t class, the type BN 1 5, was built by its parent firm of Buessing-NAG.

Some of these vehicles were modified to carry armor and to mount a high-velocity 75 mm gun in a rotating turret. Note that the muzzle brake is not mounted on this gun.

Three different versions of this vehicle existed. With a four-man crew, they were supposed to be used as an offensive weapon with cavalry units.

Built also by Buessing-NAG, they were called "7.5 cm Sf l  L/40.8" and one of these prototypes actually saw combat in North Africa.

The artillery version of the 5 t half-track was used mainly to tow the 105 mm light field howitzer.

This unit is shown during maneuvers in 1937 and provided necessary mobility for artillery units.

The cross-country ability of these vehicles was outstanding and negotiation of difficult terrain could always be accomplished.

It carried the entire gun crew, including enough ammunition to provide immediate fire protection for armored formations.

They were used in combat for the first time in Poland, where this unit is seen crossing a small river.

Some of the vehicles of the 5 t class saw service as snow plows to keep supply routes open.

An improved version of the 5 t unit appeared in 1938 and was called BN 1 8. Here it is shown with the special body for engineering outfits, where it was used mainly to tow bridging equipment.

The artillery version had lesser seating capacity but carried the usual ammunition compartment in the rear.

It still was used mainly to tow the 105 mm light field howitzer.

Army anti-aircraft units used the 5 t vehicle to mount the 37 mm Flak. It normally carried a crew of 7 and towed its own ammunition trailer.

An attempt was made to provide mobility for the 7.62 cm Russian anti-tank gun in providing a makeshift armored fighting compartment for this unit.

One of these vehicles was actually used in North Africa where it was captured by the British.

# MITTLERER, ZUGKRAFTWAGEN 5 t (Sd. Kfz. 6) Type "BN 9"

| | | | |
|---|---|---|---|
| CREW | 15 | | |
| COMBAT WEIGHT | 9000 kp | | |
| LENGTH | 6325 mm | | |
| WIDTH | 2260 mm | | |
| HEIGHT | 2500 mm | | |
| MAXIMUM SPEED | 50 km/h | | |
| MAXIMUM RANGE | 300 km | | |
| ARMAMENT | None | | |
| AMMUNITION | —— | | |
| ARMOR | FRONT | | |
| | SIDE | | |
| | TOP | = W/O | |
| | REAR | | |
| ENGINE | Maybach "HL 54 TUKRM" 6 cyl. gasoline 115 BHP | | |
| TRANSMISSION | ZF | FORWARD 4 x 2 | REVERSE 1 x 2 |
| FUEL CAPACITY | 190 Litres | | |
| TRACK WIDTH | 320 mm | | |
| MANUFACTURER | Buessing - NAG, Berlin | | |

As a replacement for the 5 t vehicles, the Schwere Wehrmachtschlepper went into production in 1943. It had a greatly-simplified suspension system. Some of these vehicles were also used as self-propelled mount for the 37 mm Flak.

## SCHWERER WEHRMACHTSSCHLEPPER Type "sWS"

| | |
|---|---|
| CREW | 12 |
| COMBAT WEIGHT | 13500 kp |
| LENGTH | 6675 mm |
| WIDTH | 2500 mm |
| HEIGHT | 2830 mm |
| MAXIMUM SPEED | 27. 4 km/h |
| MAXIMUM RANGE | 300 km |
| ARMAMENT | None |
| AMMUNITION | — — |
| ARMOR | FRONT |
| | SIDE |
| | TOP =W/O |
| | REAR |
| ENGINE | Maybach "HL 42 TRKMS" 6 cyl. gasoline 100 BHP |
| TRANSMISSION | ZF FORWARD 4 x 2 REVERSE 1 x 2 |
| FUEL CAPACITY | 240 Litres |
| TRACK WIDTH | 500 mm |
| MANUFACTURER | Buessing - NAG, Berlin - Tatra, Kolin |

To negotiate difficult terrain in Russia, large number of standard 3 t trucks were converted to half-track vehicles. They carried a modified Carden-Loyd suspension system. They were called Maultier, or Sd. Kfz. 3. Picture shows the Opel version. The same modifications also took place with Ford and Magirus vehicles.

Three hundred of the Opel vehicles were armored and served as carriers for the 15 cm Panzerwerfer 42, a rocket thrower unit, which was extensively used by the German Army.

These units provided concentrated fire power and supported advancing Panzergrenadier units substantially.

A battery of these vehicles during field exercise. Most of these units mounted an MG 42 for protection against low-flying aircraft and ground attacks.

Concluding the development of the 5 t class and serving as a stop gap until the Wehrmachtschlepper was finally available was a modification of the 5 t truck of the Daimler-Benz AG. Picture shows the vehicle with a modified suspension system, while the original half-track unit had a Panzer II suspension installed.

The first model of the 8 t series was the Krauss-Maffei vehicle appearing in 1933. It had a relatively short tracked portion of the suspension and did not provide the unit with an adequate cross-country ability.

An improved version, the KM m 9, appeared in 1935 and is shown here as a prime mover for the 88 mm Flak.

The final production model was the KM m 11, shown here in Russia pulling the 15 cm heavy field howitzer 18.

Picture shows a battery of these guns on a march. The 8 t unit is followed by a 5 t half-track vehicle.

Another scene from the Russian theater of war shows the same tractor towing 88 mm anti-aircraft guns, which were at this time quite frequently used for defense against attacking tanks. Note that during this time, many German outfits were still equipped with horses.

These guns were used substantially against armored targets and received for this purpose an armor shield.

Since the soft-skinned tractor was very vulnerable toward ground and air attacks, many attempts were made to enclose the crew compartment with an armored superstructure.

Sd. Kfz. 7/1 carried the quadruple 20 mm anti-aircraft gun 38.

Also mounted on the same chassis was the 37 mm Flak 36. The unit was called Sd. Kfz. 7/2.

Some of these vehicles had armor shields, but not just for the gun but also for the cab and engine compartment.

V-2 rocket units activated in 1944, used 8 t half-track vehicles as fire guidance centers. Picture shows one beside an erected V-2 rocket still mounted on its Meiller trailer.

To protect the crew against blast and explosion, the vehicle had received an armored superstructure holding most of the guidance equipment for the rocket.

It also towed the mobile fire platform from which the rocket was launched.

The beginning of the 12 t clas was made by the Daimler-Ben Type ZD 5, which appeared a early as 1931 and was originall intended for the Russian govern ment.

The modified version DBs 7 was used mainly by heavy artillery battalions as the standard prime mover for 15 cm guns.

It normally carried a crew of 11 and enough ammunition for immediate fire support.

This picture indicates clearly the cross-country ability of the half-track units. Vehicle shown is the Daimler-Benz type DBs 8.

xtensive troop trials substantiated e basic design and established ese vehicles as major equip-ent for the German Army.

The Daimler-Benz type DB 9 was the following model but was completely identical with its predecessors. Front and rear suspension elements can clearly be seen in this picture.

The final version called DB 10, had solid front wheel discs and is shown here negotiating difficult terrain in Russia.

They were mainly used to tow th 21 cm heavy mortar, which wa normally carried in two indepenc ent loads. Picture shows the gu combination leading a column o German transports through heav terrain.

The largest unit of the half-trac development was the 18 t Fam Sd. Kfz. 9. The picture shows a ver rare artillery version used for tov ing the 24 cm long-range gun.

Normally, the units were used as tank retrievers, where they proved to be quite adequate until the introduction of heavier vehicles in 1942. The picture shows three of the 18 t units pulling a disabled tank destroyer, Elefant.

Some of the units engaged in the pulling of tanks were equipped with large spades which helped considerably to improve the performance of their heavy winches.

Most of the time they towed an 8-wheeled trailer which could carry tanks up to 24 tons. Our picture shows a complete unit providing transportation for a Panzer III.

An attempt was made to provide mobility for the 88 mm Flak 37 when Weserhuette provided armor for some 18 t vehicles and mounted the gun in a 360° traverse. Only a few of these units were actually built.

## AN ARMOR SERIES SPECIAL

# ARMOR on the Western Desert

Volume 8, another "Armor Series Special", will feature a detailed picture coverage of the AFV's employed by the Axis and Allied Forces during the African Campaign.

52 pages 4 pages of color Over 100 photos and drawings $3.00